Perseus and Medusa

Written by C.J. Naden
Illustrated by Robert Baxter

Troll Associates

Pronunciation Guide

Acrisius	(uh-KRIS-ee-us)
Andromeda	(an-DROM-uh-duh)
Athena	(uh-THEE-nuh)
Danae	(DAN-uh-ee)
Dictys	(DIK-tus)
Electryon	(e-LEK-tree-on)
Gorgons	(GOR-gonz)
Hercules	(HUR-kyuh-leez)
Hermes	(HUR-meez)
Medusa	(me-DU-suh)
Olympus	(oh-LIM-pus)
Perseus	(PUR-see-us)
Polydectes	(pol-ee-DEK-teez)
Zeus	(ZOOSS)

The messenger ran into the palace courtyard. "A child has been born to the Princess!" he shouted. "Princess Danae has a son!" The messenger was very happy and excited about bringing such wonderful news.

But Danae's father, King Acrisius, did not think the news was wonderful. In fact, the messenger's words frightened him so that he could hardly move. Long ago, a prophet had told the King that he would be killed by his own daughter's son. Now the child was born. What could Acrisius do?

"I cannot kill my own grandson," thought Acrisius. "But I cannot let him live either!" Finally, the frightened King decided on a plan. He locked his daughter and the child in a huge chest. Then his servants tossed the chest into the sea. The King thought that the chest would sink to the bottom of the ocean.

But the King was wrong. The chest did not sink. It tossed about for days. At any moment, Danae thought that she and her child would be drowned. Instead, the chest washed ashore on an island. A fisherman named Dictys stumbled upon it. He was very surprised to find a woman and child inside.

Danae and the child, whose name was Perseus, went to live with Dictys and his wife. As the years passed, Perseus grew into a strong young man. One day the King of the island came to visit Danae. "I wish you to be my wife," said the King. Danae was not sure that she wanted to marry King Polydectes. But Perseus was very pleased. He thought it would be pleasant to live in a palace.

But Polydectes had other ideas. Vain and jealous, he certainly did not want handsome young Perseus in his court. How could he get rid of Perseus and still have Danae as his wife? An idea came to him. The King knew that Perseus was proud. He would surely want to give his mother a very special wedding gift, something that no one else could give.

So one day the King told Perseus of three monsters known as the Gorgons. "They were once beautiful women, but the gods have punished them. Now they have the bodies of huge birds with twisted claws. Snakes crawl in their hair. Only one of them — Medusa — can be killed. But many brave men have died trying to bring back her head."

Perseus did just what the King thought he would do. "I'll bring back Medusa's head as a wedding gift," he boasted. The King laughed to himself as he watched Perseus set off. No one could kill Medusa. Instead, Perseus would be killed, and the King would be rid of him.

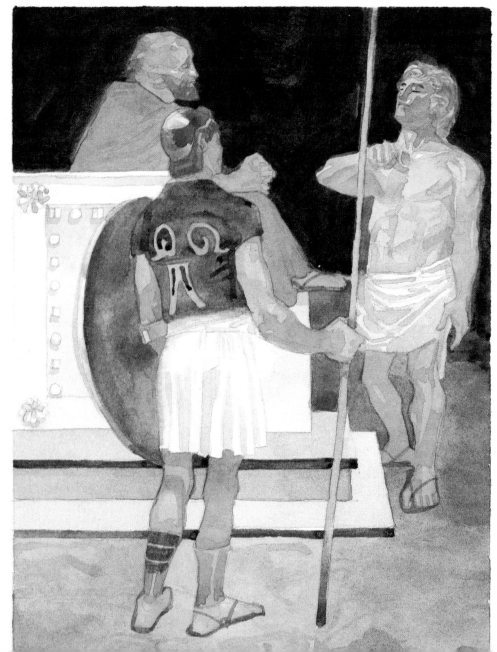

The King's plan might have worked. But Zeus, who was the ruler of all the gods and goddesses of the ancient world, decided to help Perseus. The young man did not know it, but Zeus was his father. Zeus sent Hermes, the messenger god, down from Mount Olympus. "You must have special weapons to kill Medusa," said Hermes. "Come, I know where to find the Gorgons."

Perseus was soon ready for battle. He wore winged sandals, like those of Hermes, so that he could fly. He carried a sack that could hold anything. He had a cap that would make him invisible. Hermes himself gave the young warrior a silver sword that would never break. "I will surely kill Medusa now!" cried Perseus.

But Zeus sent more help to Perseus. This time he called for Athena, the goddess of wisdom and warfare. "Take my brightly polished shield into the battle with you," Athena said. "You must never look directly into the face of a Gorgon. If you do, you will turn to stone. Look only into my shield as you attack. Use it as a mirror, and it will keep you safe."

13

Athena and Hermes led Perseus to the island where the Gorgons lived. From high in the clouds, Perseus looked down upon the hideous monsters. Their scaly bodies twisted and turned. Snakes hissed and swirled about their heads. They curled and uncurled their long thin tongues. "Remember," Athena warned again, "look only into the shield, or you will turn to stone."

Keeping his eyes on the shield, Perseus flew over the twisting, scaly body of Medusa. She looked up as though she had heard a sound. But Perseus wore his magic cap, and Medusa could not see him. Now he must strike!

Perseus tightened his hand around the silver sword and swooped down. His eyes were steady on the shield. With a quick thrust, he drove the sword into Medusa's throat. She screamed in terrible pain. Then, with a single stroke, Perseus cut off her head! Quickly he threw it into the sack. Then up he flew. His magic sandals carried him high into the air. He was out of reach of the other Gorgons.

Perseus could not believe his good luck. He had killed the hideous monster. Now he could give his mother this rarest of all gifts. "I shall never forget your help," he said to Hermes and Athena. Then he left them and began the long journey home. In the magic sack, he carried the head of Medusa.

The homeward journey was long, and Perseus was very tired. He decided to rest for a few days in a strange land. The people of this land lived in great fear of a huge sea serpent. They told Perseus that, at that very moment, the Princess Andromeda was to be sacrificed to the serpent.

Perseus went in search of the Princess. He found her chained
to a rocky ledge. She was calm and brave as she awaited her
fate. Struck by her courage as well as her beauty, Perseus fell
in love with her. He stood by her side, and together they
waited for the serpent to appear.

Slowly the waves rose higher and higher. Finally, the monster reared its ugly head above the water. It began to crawl toward the helpless Andromeda. But Perseus still carried his silver sword. And now he used it again. Just as the serpent was about to strike, Perseus cut off its head. Then he unchained Andromeda.

Perseus told the Princess of his love for her. With her father's blessing, they were married in the royal palace. Then they said farewell to the King and sailed for Perseus' home. He was anxious to see his mother, and bring her the head of Medusa. He had been gone a long time.

But when Perseus returned home, he found that many things had changed. The wife of Dictys was dead. Perseus learned that his mother had refused to marry the King. Now she feared for her life because the King had sent his soldiers to find her. She and Dictys were hiding in a temple in the country-side.

Perseus at last realized that Polydectes was an evil man. With Athena's shield in one hand and the magic sack in the other, Perseus entered the King's palace. He found Polydectes and his court enjoying a feast in the great hall. As the young man entered, the music and laughter stopped. All was silent.

The King rose from his jeweled throne, his eyes wide with surprise. But before the King could say a word, Perseus spoke. "You are an evil man, Polydectes. I know that you sent me to die." Then Perseus took the head of Medusa from the sack. He held it high in the air. Instantly, the King and all his guests turned to stone. There they would stay for all time.

Now Danae and the people of the island were free. Dictys became the new ruler. But Perseus decided to return to Greece.
Despite what had happened so many years ago, Danae wish-
ed to see her father once more. With a sad heart, Perseus said
goodbye to Dictys, the kind fisherman who had been like a
father to him.

Perseus, Andromeda, and Danae traveled to the court of King Acrisius. But he was not there. Years before, the people had tired of his evil ways and had driven him from the city. No one knew where he was or if he still lived. "I would like to see this man who is my grandfather," Perseus told Danae. And so they went in search of him.

They traveled about the country looking for the old King. But they heard no word of him. Then one day they came to a strange city. Huge crowds filled the marketplace. There was excitement in the air. "What is happening?" Perseus asked a young boy. "Today is our great athletic contest," said the boy. "The best athletes in the land are here!"

Perseus was a fine athlete himself. So he decided to enter the contest. He was skilled in racing and in the hurdles. He could wrestle and toss the javelin with the best. But he was greatest of all at throwing the discus. When his turn came, Perseus picked up the heavy discus and took a deep breath. With all his strength, he flung the discus into the air. But it did not fly straight. Instead, the discus swerved and dropped into the crowd.

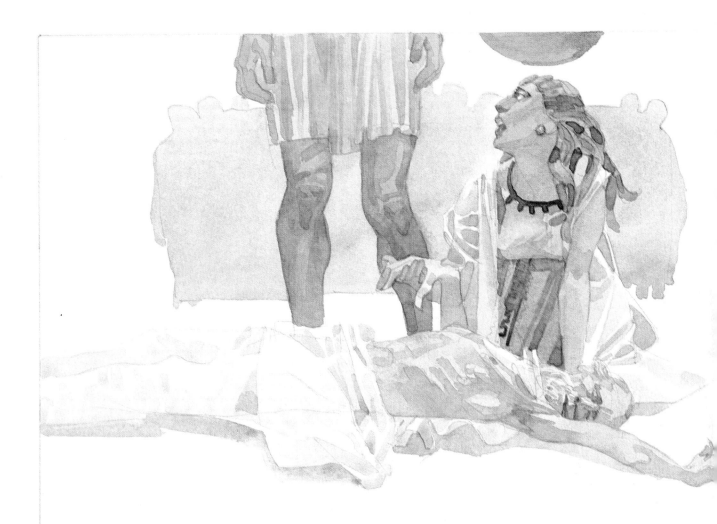

There were great cries among the spectators. The discus struck an old man in the head, killing him instantly. Perseus was horrified, and he ran to the figure on the ground. But Danae reached the old man first. She looked down at his face. Then she said to her son, "This is King Acrisius, my father."

Perseus was sick with grief. "I have killed my grandfather!" he cried. But Danae said to him, "No, no, my son. It was not your doing. The words of the old prophet have come true. It is the will of the gods."

Perseus, Andromeda, and Danae returned to the King's court. Perseus now wore the crown that had been his grandfather's. He was a good and wise ruler, and he and Andromeda lived together in happiness for many years. In time they had a son called Electryon. He would become the grandfather of the greatest of all heroes of Greece — Hercules.

Perseus returned the silver sword to Athena. He gave her the head of Medusa as well. Athena placed Medusa's head on the front of her shield. It remained there for all time. The head of Medusa became a sign of great power. It would forever be a threat to all those who were evil or unjust.